How It All Began!

The Creation and Expansion of British Colonies in America

NORTH AMERICAN COLONIZATION 3RD GRADE | CHILDREN'S AMERICAN HISTORY

First Edition, 2021

Published in the United States by Speedy Publishing LLC, 40 E Main Street, Newark, Delaware 19711 USA.

© 2021 Baby Professor Books, an imprint of Speedy Publishing LLC

All rights reserved.

Without limiting the rights under the copyright reserved above, no part of this publication may be reproduced, stored in or introduced into a retrieval system, or transmitted, in any form, or by any means (electronic, mechanical, photocopying, recording, or otherwise), without the prior written permission of the copyright owner.

All images in this book have been reproduced with the knowledge and prior consent of the artists concerned, and no responsibility is accepted by producer, publisher, or printer for any infringement of copyright or otherwise arising from the contents of this publication.

Baby Professor Books are available at special discounts when purchased in bulk for industrial and sales-promotional use. For details contact our Special Sales Team at Speedy Publishing LLC, 40 E Main Street, Newark, Delaware 19711 USA. Telephone (888) 248-4521 Fax: (210) 519-4043.

10 9 8 7 6 * 5 4 3 2 1

Print Edition: 9781541978515
Digital Edition: 9781541978652
Hardcover Edition: 9781541983588

See the world in pictures. Build your knowledge in style.
www.speedypublishing.com

Table of Contents

Chapter One:
The Thirteen Colonies 9

Chapter Two:
New York, New Jersey, and Delaware 31

Chapter Three:
The Carolinas 57

Do you know how many states make up the United States of America? If your answer is fifty, then you are correct. Do you know that at one time, there were no states at all? At one time, the North American continent was inhabited by native groups of people. It later saw the arrival of people from different European countries.

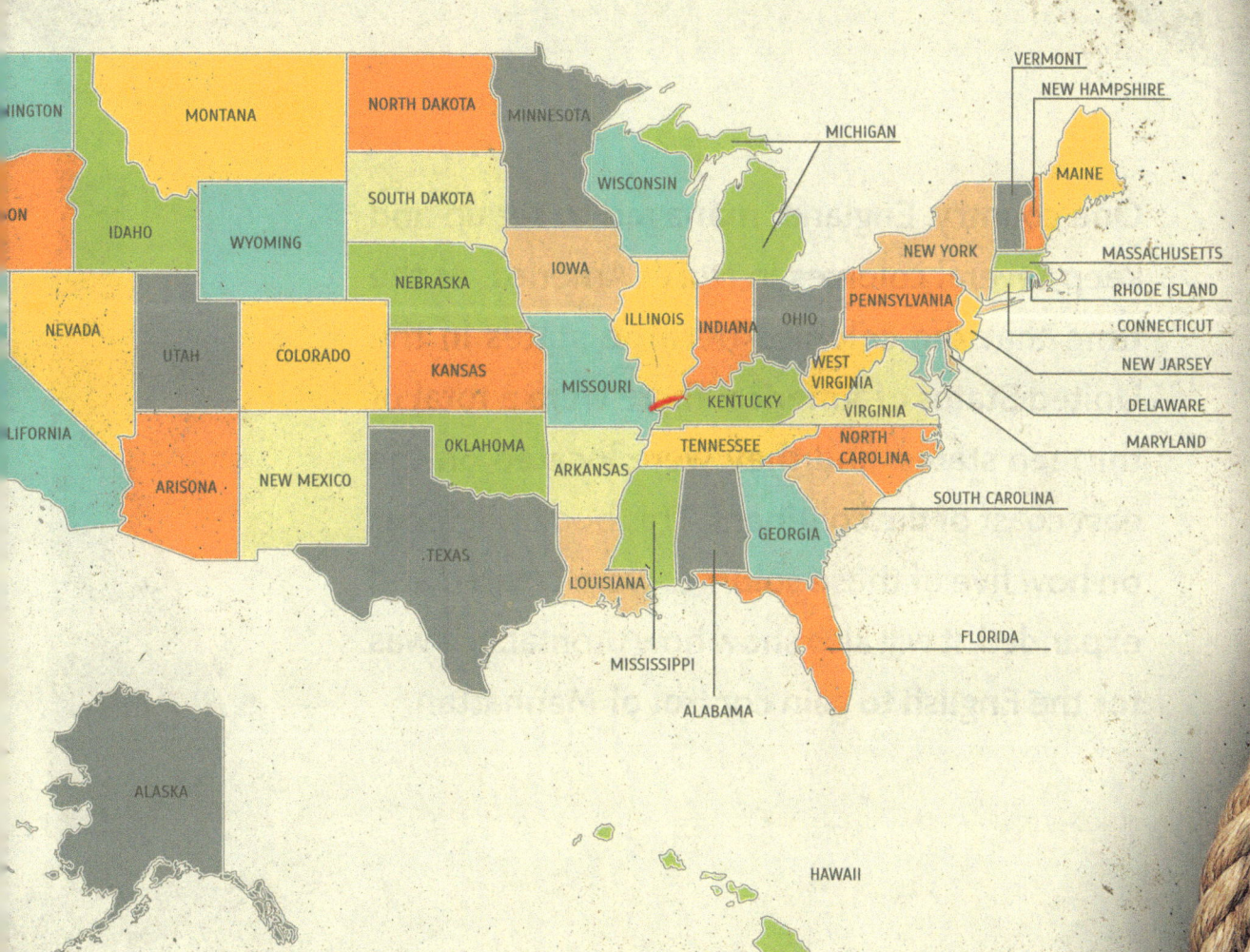

Map of the United States of America

One country, England, managed to set up and keep several colonies in North America. At the time that the colonies became states in the United States of America, there were a total of thirteen states, and they were located on the east coast of the continent. This book will focus on how five of these colonies were created and expanded. It will also show how profitable it was for the English to gain control of Manhattan.

England managed to set up and keep several colonies in North America.

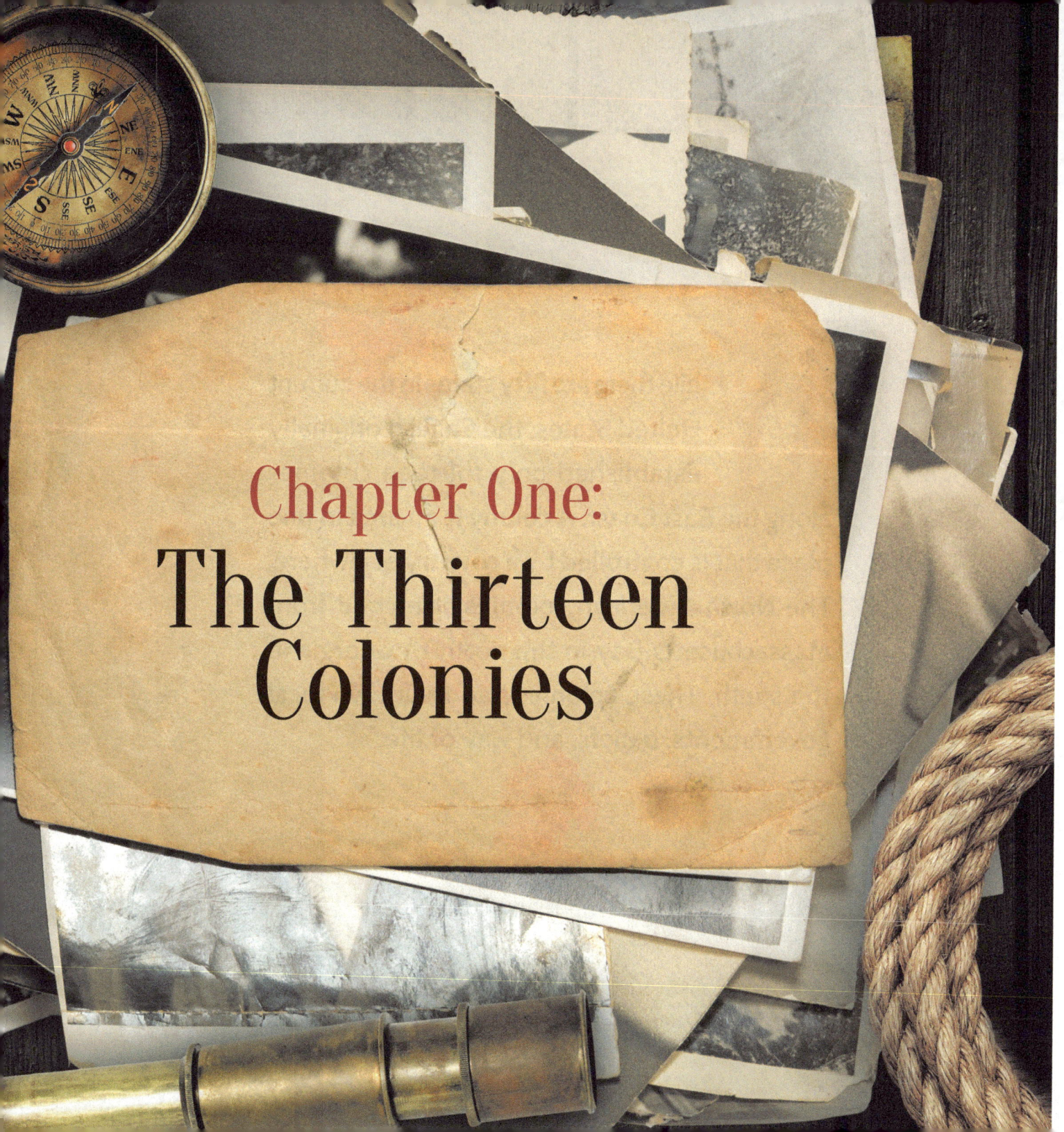

Chapter One:
The Thirteen Colonies

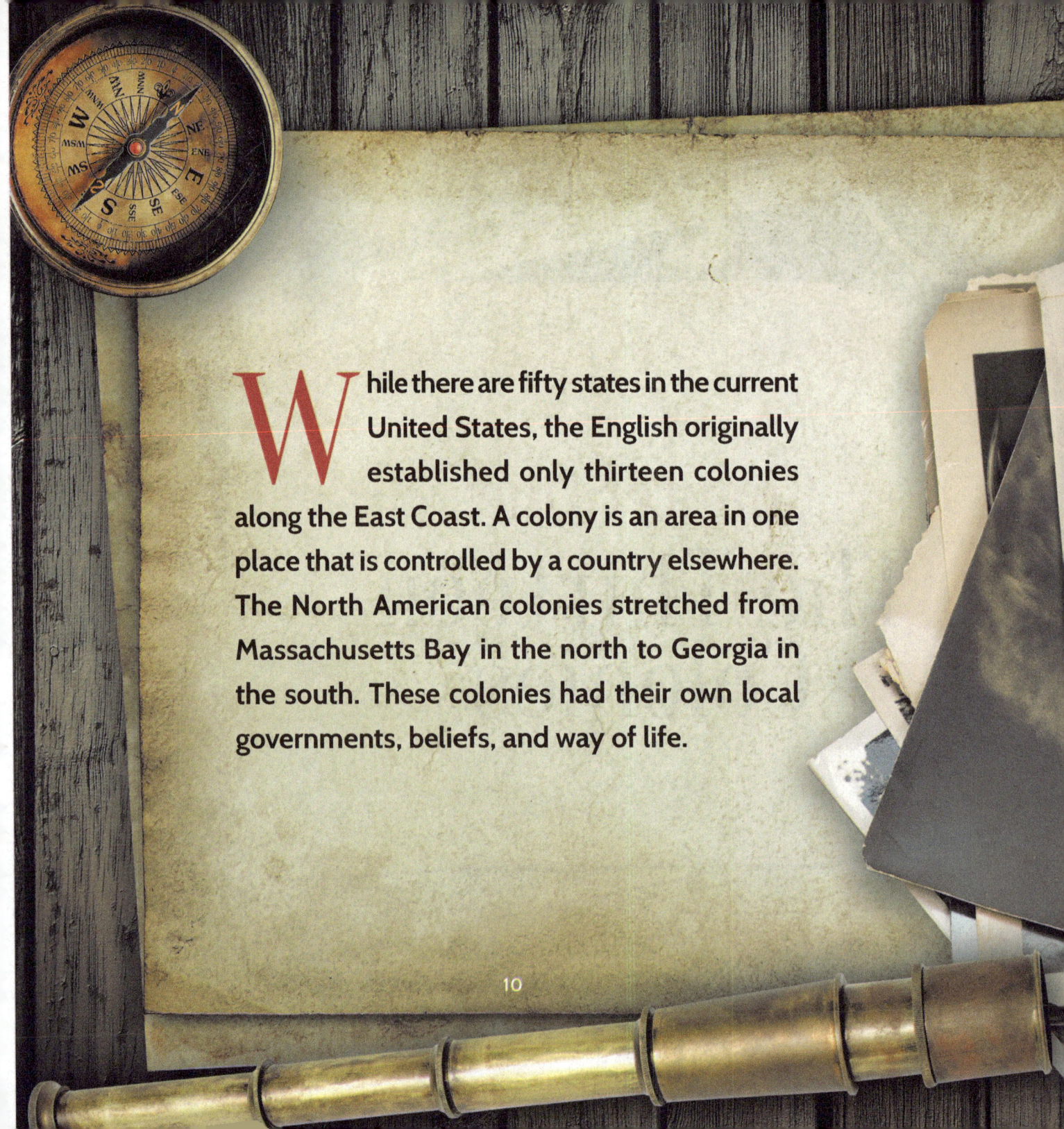

While there are fifty states in the current United States, the English originally established only thirteen colonies along the East Coast. A colony is an area in one place that is controlled by a country elsewhere. The North American colonies stretched from Massachusetts Bay in the north to Georgia in the south. These colonies had their own local governments, beliefs, and way of life.

Map of the original 13 colonies

Colonial Government:

The British did not settle all the colonies at once. The settlements happened gradually over the course of a century. Additionally, the control over the colonies was not always in the total control of the hands of the English. New York, for instance, was once called New Amsterdam and was under the control of the Dutch.

Dutch colony of New Amsterdam showing the fort, the wall, windmill, church, and pillory in 1659.

France also held a lot of territory in Canada and when a dispute erupted over the ownership of the Ohio Valley, there was a war called the French and Indian War. When the English won the war, they were finally able to ensure their own control over the original thirteen colonies that they had there.

The Siege of Louisbourg was a pivotal battle of the French and Indian War, which ended the French colonial era.

Many of the colonists who traveled from England to North America to live went to escape religious persecution. In England at the time, there was no religious freedom. If a person were a citizen, that person was expected to be a member of the Church of England. If somebody happened to disagree with the teachings of this church, or were part of another religion, this person would be treated badly.

Many of the colonists who traveled from England to North America to live went to escape religious persecution.

The person would get mocked, be called names, could risk losing his or her job, or even be sent to prison! After the colonists arrived in North America, having witnessed what it was like for people to live through this type of persecution, many chose to make it illegal to harass people over their religious beliefs.

If somebody happened to be part of another religion, this person would be treated badly and would be sent to prison.

Consequently, many of the colonists started to lose loyalty to the English government. To make matters worse, the English government started to enforce other laws that the colonists believed to be unjust and unfair. For example, as England continued to levy taxes on the colonists to help pay for things like the French and Indian War, the colonists decided it was time to overthrow English rule.

Riots at Boston in 1765-66 in opposition to the Stamp Act.

They believed that they had the right to govern themselves. They strongly disagreed with being taxed by a government across the Atlantic Ocean without representation in that government. When the thirteen colonies won the war, the United States was founded.

Evacuation Day on November 25 marks the day in 1783 when the British Army departed from New York City on Manhattan Island, after the end of the American Revolutionary War.

Life in the Colonies:

Most colonists who came over to North America were farmers. The colonists had to build up a community almost entirely from scratch. This meant that they could not just run to a grocery store. They would have to grow their own food and hunt down their own meat. The towns that made up the colonies would have initially been quite small.

The colonists would have to grow their own food.

In the southern colonies, farms called plantations were common. Plantations were massive farms that could produce food and crops for large profit. Tobacco and cotton crops are two examples of what was commonly grown.

A 19th century cotton plantation on the Mississippi River.

Since the farms were so big, they could not easily be run by one colonial family. Instead, slaves would be bought to help run the plantation. These slaves were considered property. They would not be paid and would often be treated terribly by their oppressive owners. Plantation owners often became quite wealthy and many were involved in the local governments.

African American slaves picking cotton in the South.

Three of the English colonies were New York, New Jersey, and Delaware. All three of these colonies were originally founded by people other than the English. However, the English would end up taking control of them. New York was a colony that granted the English a great deal of wealth.

The landing of British troops in New York.

A Brief History of New York:

The first Europeans to settle in the area that is now New York were the Dutch. They arrived in the early 1600s. They would name the area New Amsterdam in honor of the city of Amsterdam in the Netherlands. When the Dutch arrived, they established Fort Orange which is now the state capital of New York, Albany.

The Landing of the Dutch colonists known as Walloons in New Amsterdam in the 1600s.

While the Dutch controlled the area, Peter Minuit was able to buy Manhattan Island from the Algonquin Indians. He is said to have given them trinkets worth sixty Dutch coins, or twenty-four dollars. Twenty-four dollars in the 17th century was worth much more than twenty-four dollars is today. Even so, it was a profitable deal for the Dutch.

Peter Minuit purchased Manhattan Island from the Algonquin Indians for $24 worth of trinkets.

The Dutch would continue to trade with the Native population, and the Hudson River allowed them to travel and trade easily. The fur trade was known to be lucrative. Eventually, the area proved to be a significant enough source of wealth, and in such a strategic area with British colonies to the north and south, that the British decided that they wanted it.

Dutch merchants trading with Native Americans.

The British would send a fleet to New Amsterdam in 1664. Peter Stuyvesant was the governor there at the time. He knew that the Dutch could not hope to match the British and so he decided to surrender the city. It was named New York in honor of the Duke of York, the English king's brother, who oversaw the assault.

Peter Stuyvesant surrendering New Amsterdam to the English in 1664.

New York City would continue to grow as a trade center and by 1790 would be the largest city in the newly founded United States of America. The Erie Canal which connected New York City to the Great Lakes was completed in 1825. The city would then become a key seaport.

The Erie Canal took eight years to build and when completed in 1825 it opened the Great Lakes and Northwest Territory to trade and emigrants.

Ellis Island became the main entry point for people who wanted to immigrate to the United Stated. In the 19th and 20th centuries, millions of immigrants moved to New York City via Ellis Island.

IMMIGRANTS, ELLIS ISLAND

European immigrants arriving at Ellis Island, ca. 1907.

The main immigration building on Ellis Island in New York harbor.

In the modern age, New York City continues to be a vibrant and diverse city. People from many different ethnic backgrounds make this place their home. In addition, the city is home to the United Nations, and it is known for being an economic center. Economics refers to the trading, transferring, making, and consumption of wealth. New York City has come a long way from being an area occupied by a forest!

New York City, USA

New Jersey and Delaware Become English Colonies:

The Hudson River is west of Manhattan Island. Further west than the Hudson River is another large area of land called New Jersey. New Jersey was also taken over by the British from the Dutch in 1664.

A view of Jersey City, New Jersey and the Hudson River.

The Duke of York decided to divide the land between two men who were good friends. These men were Sir George Carteret and Lord Berkeley. Both these men hoped to make a lot of money off their new land. Carteret would name his land New Jersey since he was the governor of the Isle of Jersey in England.

Lord Berkeley — Sir George Carteret

Delaware was not an easy colony to establish. It too was taken by the British in the year of 1664. However, it was originally under Swedish rule, as the Swedes were the first to establish a permanent colony in the area. In 1638, they founded Fort Christina there. Today it is called Wilmington.

Swedish colonists landing at Paradise Point on the Atlantic shore of Delaware in the 1600s.

Later, in 1655, the Dutch would come and take over the area from the Swedes. In fact, the Dutch had never truly acknowledged Swedish rule of the area. The Swedes may have been the first to establish a permanent colony, but the Dutch had been visiting the area from around 1631. They failed to settle there, however, when the settlers were all killed by the Native Americans within a year. After all that, the English would take it over in 1664 and by 1701, Delaware would be considered an independent colony.

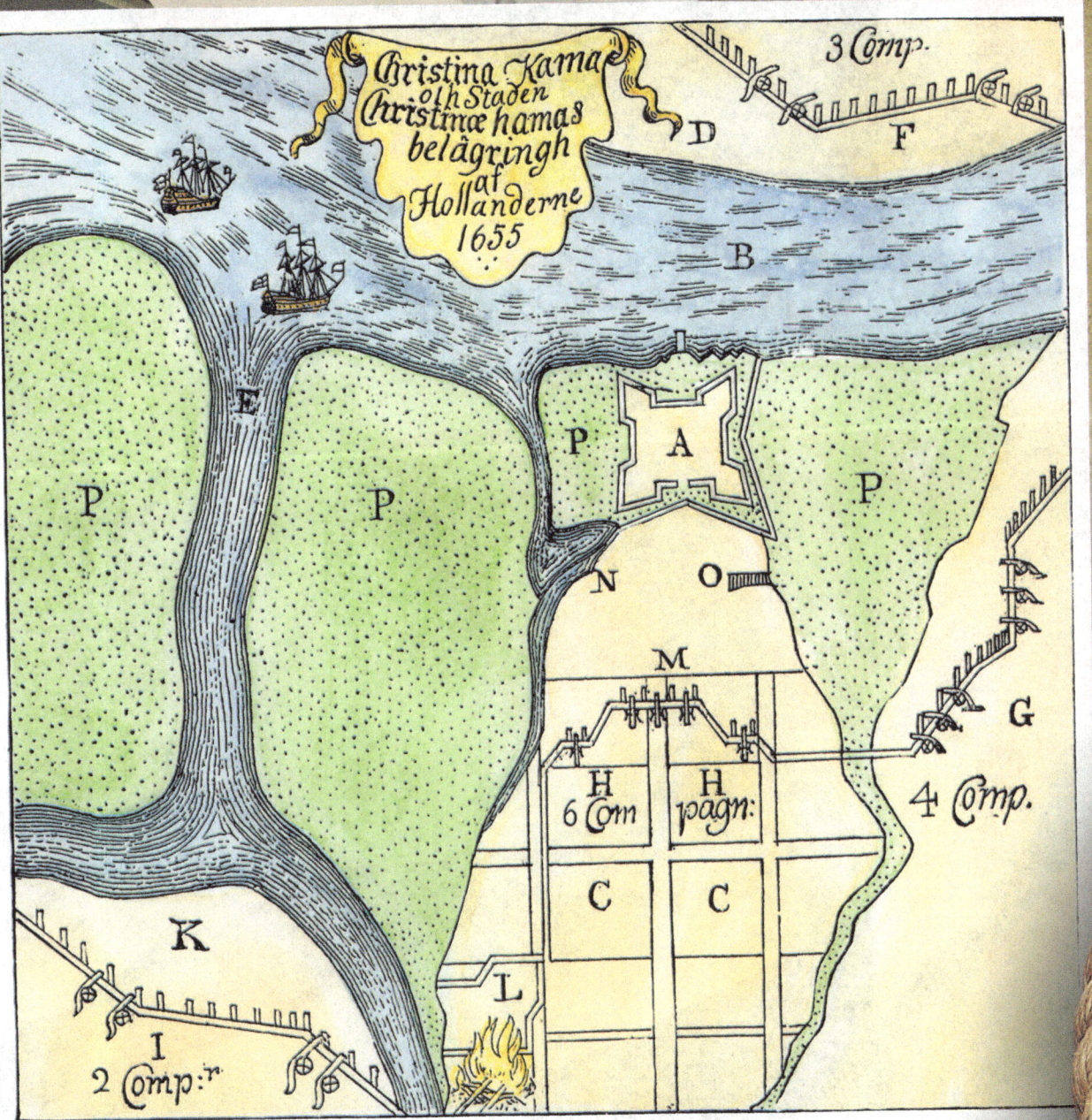

Fort Christina under siege by the Dutch in 1655, now Wilmington, Delaware.

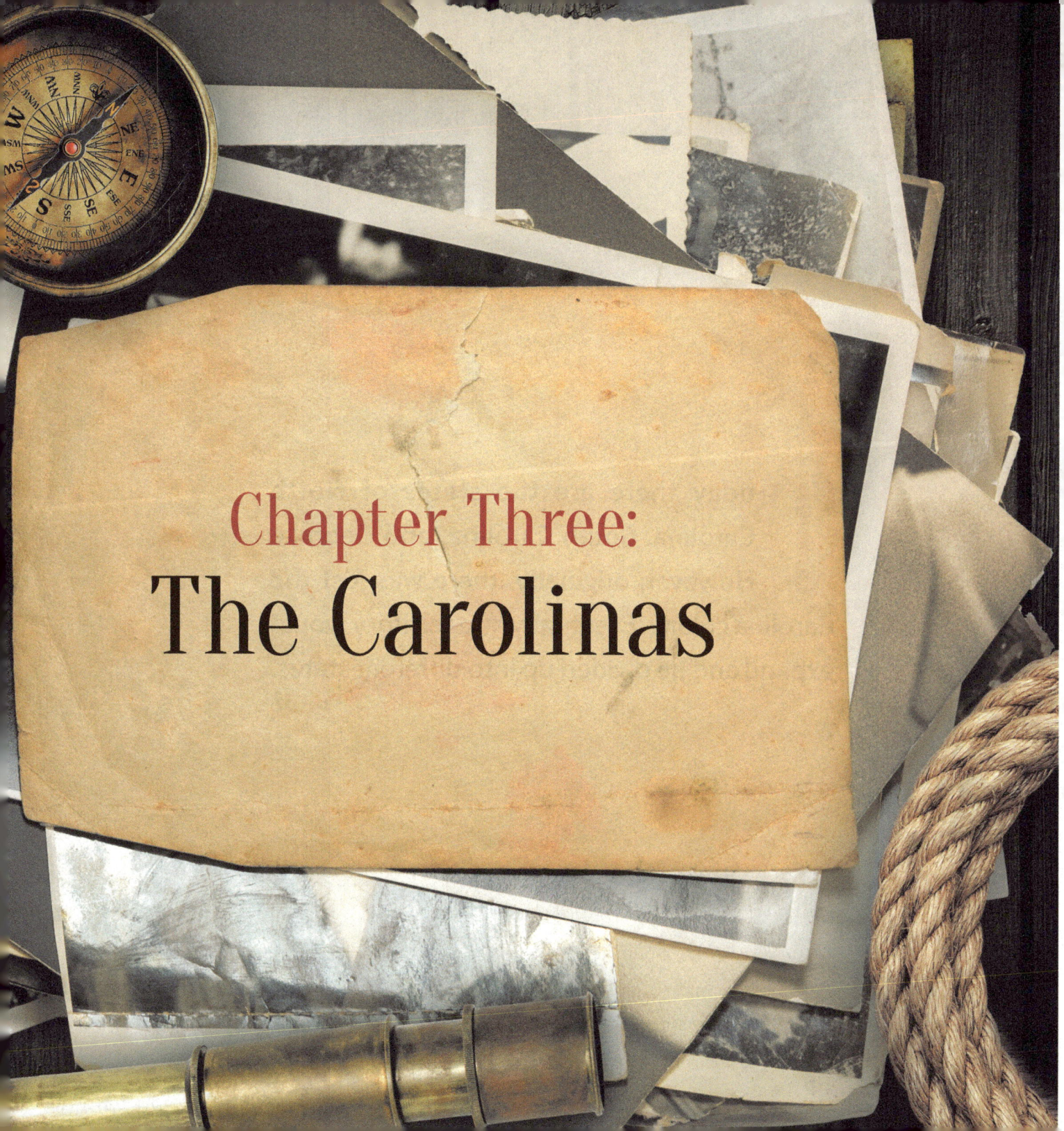

Chapter Three:
The Carolinas

Today there are the states of North Carolina, South Carolina, and Georgia. However, originally, there was just the Carolina colony. Eventually, the territory would expand and be divided up into different states.

The Carolina colony was divided up into North Carolina, South Carolina, and Georgia.

Carolina:

Carolina became a colony when King Charles I of England chose to give the land to a man who named it in his honor. The land was found south of the Virginia Colony. Colonists from Virginia had moved down there and called it Albemarle. In 1665, the charter was altered slightly under King Charles II such that the land around Albemarle became a part of Carolina.

King Charles I of England

King Charles II of England

The development of the Carolina Colony happened in such a way that most people lived in either northern Carolina or southern Carolina. Many people began to think of the Carolina colony in terms of North Carolina and South Carolina.

Settlers planting crops in South Carolina during colonial days.

Both the north and the south had their own local governments. However, they were placed under one governor in 1691. It was not until 1729 that the colony was formally divided into North Carolina and South Carolina.

A settler's cabin in North Carolina Colony.

The Founding of Georgia:

Georgia is located to the south of South Carolina. Before it was founded, however, parts of the land that now lie in Georgia were a part of South Carolina. Georgia would be founded in 1732 when King George II gave a charter for a new colony to a group led by James Edward Oglethorpe. Oglethorpe named the land Georgia in honor of the king.

King George II

The landing of James Edward Oglethorpe in colonial Georgia.

The reason for founding Georgia was strategic. The Spanish had control of Florida and the French controlled New Orleans. By founding Georgia, the British hoped to keep the French and the Spanish from expanding their territories. They also hoped that Georgia could protect the other colonists.

By founding Georgia, the British hoped to keep the French and the Spanish from expanding their territories.

At one time, the only people who inhabited the continent of North America were different groups of Native Americans. Later, when different European countries started to sail around the world, people from Europe decided to remain in North America. Before the United States of America became an official independent country, it consisted of colonies. New York, New Jersey, Delaware, the Carolinas, and Georgia were some of the first areas that were under English rule. For more information about the history and way of living in North American colonies, look for more Baby Professor books!

Made in the USA
Coppell, TX
18 January 2025